Unfindable

A Lottery Winner's Disappearance

George Hatcher

CasaHatcherPress

Printed in the United States of America and abroad.

This book can be purchased at over 44,000 bookstores and libraries, including brick-and-mortar stores and digital retailers such as Apple Books and Kindle.

Publisher:

Casa Hatcher Press, a Pretty Face, Inc. company

Rancho Mirage, California

Book Title: Unfindable: A Lottery Winner's Disappearance

by George Hatcher

eBook ISBN: 979-8-9996764-6-7

Paperback ISBN: 979-8-9996764-3-6

LCCN: Pending Jan 2026

Dedication

For Molly,

In a life filled with fleeting fireworks, you have always been the steady pilot light—the quiet flame that keeps me warm and guides me home.

Thank you for being the gold that fills all my broken places.

All my love, always,

George

Also By George Hatcher

Mario Series:

Mario 1: Woman in Jeopardy

Mario 2: Coming of Age

Mario 3: Risky Business

Mario 4: Free Fall

Mario 5: Afire

Mario 6: Marked

Mario 7: Aftershock

Mario 8: Captivated

Single Titles:

One Wilshire

Gabi

Rico

Cats: Meow Is the Language of Love

HER: Artistic Expressions Through AI

Elegance in White: Through Wedding Gowns

Quinceañera Fashion: Fifteen & Fabulous

Billion Dollar Rainmaker Series:

Billion Dollar Rainmaker Part I

Pages of Passion Series:

Pages of Passion Book 1: My First 19 Years

Pages of Passion Book 2: Bold Beginnings

Pages of Passion Book 3: Rising Waves

Pages of Passion Book 4: Threads of Destiny

Non-Fiction / Other Works:

Beyond the Scale: Health Benefits of Keto for Wellness

Cool Under Pressure: Warm with Humor

Love Is What It Is: Lessons from Everyday Life

Living Fully While We Wait to Die: Mindfulness Amid Mortality

Ignite Your Potential: Break Free from the Ordinary

AfterLight: A Voice Beyond the Grave

Coming Soon

Chapter 1

The moment the World Ended (and Began)

TICKET TO MADNESS

He checked the numbers once.

Then again, slower, with the kind of deliberate terror people use when they're defusing a bomb they accidentally built themselves.

04 ... 19 ... 27 ... 35 ... 42 ... 58.

Powerball: 12.

The room didn't spin. It detonated.

The ticket left his fingers like it was on fire, then he snatched it back, afraid the air itself might steal it. His knees buckled. A sound came out of him that wasn't a word, wasn't even human; just raw voltage ripping through vocal cords. He raised the slip of thermal paper above his head with both trembling hands, a high priest of dumb luck, and screamed until his throat tasted like copper.

Twenty-three million dollars.

After taxes, still enough to burn the old life to the ground and salt the earth.

He laughed. He cried. He laughed again until the crying took over and he couldn't tell which was which. The cheap apartment walls shook with it. Somewhere down the hall, Mrs. Delgado banged a broom against her ceiling—his floor—and yelled something about the police. He didn't care. He was untouchable now. He was radioactive.

The ticket fluttered in his grip like a white flag of surrender to a future that hadn't asked if he was ready.

He wasn't.

But ready or not, the madness had already bought its one-way ticket.

* * *

The phone was in his hand before he remembered reaching for it.

His thumb hovered over "Mom."

No. Not yet.

She'd cry, then she'd pray, then she'd tell Aunt Carla, and within thirty minutes the entire family WhatsApp would be a war zone of praise-hands emojis and GoFundMe links disguised as birthday lists.

He scrolled to "Dylan—DO NOT ANSWER."

His oldest friend. The one person who'd believe this without demanding a photo of the ticket first.

It rang once.

"Yo, what's up, loser?"

"I'm rich," he blurted. The words tasted like champagne and gasoline.

Silence. Then Dylan laughed the way people do when they think you're high. "Cool story. You hit the scratch-off for twenty bucks again?"

"Twenty-three million, Dylan. Powerball. I'm holding it right now."

Another beat of silence, longer this time. He could almost hear the exact moment his friend's brain blue-screened.

"You're fucking with me."

"I wish I was. I'm actually scared."

The laugh that came through the speaker was too loud, too sharp, the sound of someone realizing the rules just changed for both of them.

"Bro... where are you right now?"

"Still in the apartment. I—I haven't moved in like ten minutes. My legs forgot how."

"Don't move. Lock the door. Put that ticket in your mouth if you have to, just don't lose it. I'm coming over."

"You can't tell anyone."

"I'm not an idiot. Ten minutes."

The call ended.

He stared at the black screen, then at the ticket still pinched between his fingers like a hostage note.

Lock the door. Good advice.

He walked to the deadbolt on legs that felt borrowed. The chain rattled like cheap jewelry. When it was secure, he pressed his forehead to the cool metal and whispered the only sane sentence left in his head:

"What the fuck do I do now?"

Outside, a siren Dopplered past, close enough to make his heart sprint again. He flinched so hard the ticket almost slipped. He caught it against his chest, crumpling it slightly, then smoothed it out on the door like it was made of butterfly wings.

Twenty-three million dollars and the first thing he did was apologize to a piece of paper.

The madness was already winning.

The next nine minutes were the longest of his life.

He paced the six steps from the couch to the kitchenette and back, counting them like a prisoner. Every footfall sounded too loud. Every car that slowed outside might be someone who already knew. He kept the ticket in his left hand now, clenched so tight the edges cut, refusing to put it down even to wipe the sweat off his palm.

His phone buzzed. Unknown number. He almost threw it across the room.

Then the knock: three fast, two slow. Their old code from high-school parties when parents came home early.

He yanked the door open just enough to drag Dylan inside by the hoodie.

Dylan's eyes were saucers. "Let me see it, man. Now."

He opened his fist like he was revealing plutonium. The ticket trembled between them.

Dylan took it with reverent fingers, held it to the light, then looked up with an expression somewhere between terror and the purest joy a human face can hold.

"Holy... you actually did it." His voice cracked on the last word. "You're disgusting levels of rich."

"Don't say it out loud," he hissed, slamming the door and throwing the chain again.

"Too late. I'm already thinking about yachts." Dylan spun the ticket once, then handed it back like it might explode. "We gotta get you out of here. Tonight."

"Tonight?"

"People talk. The store that sold it already knows. By morning half the city's gonna be circling this building like sharks. You're not safe here."

He looked around at the sagging couch, the pizza boxes, the single sad houseplant he'd been meaning to water for three months.

"I've lived here four years."

"And now you never have to again. Congratulations, you're homeless in the best way possible."

His phone buzzed again. Same unknown number. This time it left a voicemail.

He stared at the screen like it was a loaded gun.

Dylan raised an eyebrow. "You gonna listen to that?"

"No."

"Good instinct."

Another buzz. Text this time, from a number with no name:

Congrats on the big win!! Family is so proud. Call us! We love you!!

Cousin Marco. The one who still owed him $400 from 2022.

He felt the walls tilt.

Dylan grabbed his shoulders. "Look at me. First rule of sudden money: nobody gets to celebrate with you until you decide they do. Not family, not friends, not me if I start acting weird. You understand?"

He nodded, numb.

"Second rule: we need a plan before the sun comes up. Hotel suite, paid in cash, new phone, lawyer on speed-dial. Then we figure out how to keep you alive and not completely insane."

"Too late for the insane part."

Dylan grinned, wild and sudden. "Then let's be insane together. Grab whatever you can't live without. We're leaving in sixty seconds."

He looked around the apartment one last time. Laptop. Charger. The beat-up sneakers that still had decent soles. The rest could burn.

As he stuffed it all into a backpack, Dylan was already at the window, peering through the blinds.

"Clear for now. But I swear that white van just did its third loop."

He zipped the bag, slipped the ticket into the hidden inside pocket, and zipped that twice.

Dylan clapped him on the back. "Welcome to the first night of the rest of your life, millionaire."

He laughed. One short, cracked sound that hurt coming out.

"Let's go," he said.

They stepped into the hallway and pulled the door shut behind them, the click of the lock sounding weirdly final.

A new life was waiting.

So was everyone else.

Unfindable

* * *

They took the stairs because the elevator felt like a coffin with fluorescent lighting.

Third floor, second floor, first; every footstep echoed like a gunshot. Dylan moved like he'd done this before, which he hadn't, but adrenaline is a hell of a director. At the lobby door he held up a fist (old war-movie bullshit) and peeked through the glass.

"Van's gone. Coast is clear. We go fast, we go quiet. My car's half a block north."

He nodded, mouth dry. The ticket pressed against his ribs through the backpack strap like a second heartbeat.

They slipped outside. Night air hit him like cold water. The street was ordinary (same cracked sidewalk, same flickering liquor-store sign), but everything looked fake now, like a stage set someone forgot to strike.

Dylan's beat-up Civic sat under a broken streetlight. Perfect.

They were ten feet away when headlights flared behind them.

White van. No plates on the front.

It rolled slow, window halfway down, phone flashlight glowing inside like a single evil eye.

Dylan didn't hesitate. "Run."

They sprinted. Keys jangled. Doors unlocked with that pathetic beep-beep that suddenly sounded like a dinner bell. He threw himself into the passenger seat as Dylan cranked the engine.

The van crawled closer, lazy, confident, like it already knew where they lived.

Dylan reversed hard, tires chirping, then slammed it into drive and punched the gas. The Civic fishtailed, caught traction, and shot forward.

In the side mirror he watched the van sit there for a second, then flip a lazy U-turn and fade into the night.

Neither of them spoke until they hit the highway on-ramp doing seventy.

Only then did Dylan let out a shaky laugh. "Welcome to the big leagues, bro. Population: you, me, and every scavenger with a police scanner."

He stared straight ahead, fingers digging into the seatbelt across his chest like it was the only thing keeping his organs inside.

"Hotel?" he asked.

"Already booked two rooms under my mom's maiden name. Cash deposit tomorrow morning. We'll switch again at noon. And we're buying you a hat and sunglasses that scream 'I'm absolutely not a millionaire.'"

He almost smiled. Almost.

His phone buzzed again. Another unknown number. This time a photo message.

He opened it before he could stop himself.

A grainy picture of the apartment building's front door. Taken less than five minutes ago.

Underneath, three words:

We see you.

He turned the screen off so fast the glass squeaked.

Dylan glanced over. "What was it?"

"Nothing," he lied. First lie of the new life. It tasted metallic, like blood.

The highway lights strobed across the windshield, faster and faster, until the whole world blurred into white streaks.

Ticket to madness, indeed.

He closed his eyes and waited for the next exit, the next lie, the next heartbeat that might not actually belong to him anymore.

Chapter 2

The Motel That Smelled Like Old Cigarettes and New Fear

The room was number 212, second floor, far end, the one with the view of the dumpster and the flickering "VACANCY" sign that only lit the "VAC" part anymore. Perfect.

Dylan dropped the duffel, killed the overhead light, and left only the weak amber glow from the bathroom bleeding across the carpet. He pulled the baseball bat (aluminum, scuffed to hell from high-school days) out of his backpack like it was Excalibur and took position by the window, one finger nudging the curtain a millimeter.

Our winner sat on the edge of the bed that sagged in the middle like it had given up years ago. The ticket was out of the backpack now, sealed inside a Ziploc bag he'd found in Dylan's glove box, then tucked into the pocket of his hoodie. It pressed against his heart with every breath. He could feel the numbers through two layers of plastic and cotton: 04-19-27-35-42-58. A tattoo he hadn't asked for.

Dylan whispered without turning. "You breathing?"

"Barely."

"Good. Keep it that way."

Silence stretched, thick and cheap as the comforter. The ice machine down the hall clunked and gurgled like it was choking on its own cubes.

He pulled out the new burner phone (sixty bucks cash at a 24-hour Walmart, still in the plastic clamshell). He hadn't turned it on yet. Turning it on felt like lighting a flare in a dark forest full of wolves.

"Do it," Dylan said, reading his mind the way only twenty-year friendships allow. "You need to know how bad it is."

He cracked the plastic, slid the battery in, watched the screen bloom to life. No SIM yet. Safe. He connected to the motel's free Wi-Fi (password "guest1234," because of course it was) and opened an incognito tab.

Typed his own name.

The results loaded like a punch in the throat.

First hit: a local news site, posted forty-three minutes ago.

"$23 Million Powerball Ticket Sold at Eastside Convenience – Winner Still Unknown"

Second hit: a Facebook group already created, 2,847 members and climbing.

"Who won the Powerball on Eastside???"

Third hit: a blurry photo of the exact convenience store counter where he'd bought the ticket, timestamped tonight.

Someone had circled the clerk in red and written "HE KNOWS."

His hands started shaking so hard the phone screen wobbled.

Dylan glanced over. "That fast?"

"Faster."

"Close it."

He did. The screen went black, but the afterimage of those headlines stayed burned on his retinas.

He set the phone face-down on the nightstand like it was radioactive.

Dylan finally turned from the window. "Tomorrow we get you to a lawyer who does this for a living. Guy charges five grand just to walk in the door, but he'll set up blindsided trusts or whatever so nobody can find you. After that, we disappear you for a month. Maybe two."

"Disappear me where?"

"Somewhere with no people and a lot of ocean. I'm thinking we start with a map and a dartboard."

He laughed. Couldn't help it. One cracked, desperate sound.

Then the laugh died.

Because the burner phone buzzed.

One single buzz. A text.

From a number that was just zeros: 000-000-0000.

The message was three words and a photo.

Unfindable

We never left.

The photo: the motel parking lot, taken from the shadows near the dumpster. Dylan's Civic clear as day, license plate perfectly readable.

Time stamp: thirty-seven seconds ago.

Dylan saw his face drain of blood and was at the window in one silent stride, bat raised. The curtain moved a fraction.

Nothing out there but sodium light and empty spaces.

He eased the curtain shut again and looked at the phone like it had teeth.

"Turn it off," he whispered.

He did.

Then he pulled the battery out for good measure and set both pieces on the carpet like they might still bite.

Dylan exhaled through his teeth. "New rule. From now on, nobody sleeps."

He looked at the bat, then at his best friend, then at the door that suddenly felt made of paper.

"Fine," he said. "But if nobody sleeps, somebody pours the whiskey."

Dylan actually grinned at that. A small, feral thing.

He reached into the duffel and pulled out the half-empty bottle of Jack they'd bought with the burner phone.

"Welcome to night one, millionaire-in-hiding," he said, twisting the cap. "Drink fast. The sun's gonna rat us out in four hours."

He took the bottle with both shaking hands and drank until it burned worse than the fear.

Outside, the ice machine clunked again, and somewhere in the dark, something that already knew his name waited for morning.

Chapter 3

Dawn Tastes Like Copper and Burnt Coffee

The lawyer's office didn't have a sign. Just a steel door in a brick building that used to be a dry-cleaner. Dylan had found him the way people find organ donors: dark web forum, three referrals, one whispered phone call at 5:12 a.m.

The man who opened the door wore a charcoal suit and the exhausted calm of someone who'd hidden rap sheets and rape charges and now, apparently, lottery winners. No small talk. He looked at the Ziplock bag our winner held out like a heart in a cooler.

"Name on the ticket?" he asked.

"Doesn't matter yet."

"Good answer. Come in."

Inside smelled like lemon polish and paranoia. Blinds drawn tight. A single chair in front of a desk that probably cost more than the building.

The lawyer (call me Roth) slid over a thick stack of forms and a pen that wrote like it had secrets.

"Sign nothing with your real name. We're creating a blind trust in the Caymans today. You'll claim the prize through a limited liability company owned by another limited liability company owned by a trust that doesn't have your birthday in it. By the time anyone finishes peeling the onion, you'll be a ghost who happens to own half of South Dakota."

He stared at the first blank line.

Roth kept talking, soft and fast. "Lump sum is 23.4 million before taxes. After federal withholding you walk with roughly 16.8. State tax takes another bite. You'll clear about 14.2 when the check finally lands. Still enough to make people kill you in your sleep, so we don't let the check land in your name."

He signed where the finger pointed. The pen felt heavier than the bat.

Roth took the forms, slid them into a folder marked only with a six-digit number.

"Second thing. You're about to become the most photographed man in the state the second you step into that claim center. We don't let that happen."

He looked up. "How?"

Roth opened a drawer and took out a driver's license. Same photo as his real one, different name, different birthdate, address in Wyoming.

"Tomorrow morning you fly to Des Moines. Private charter, cash. You claim the prize wearing a baseball cap, sunglasses, and forty extra pounds we're going to glue to your face with spirit gum and bad decisions. You'll look like a depressed trucker named Dale Schroeder. Dale has a lawyer (me) and Dale doesn't speak to cameras. You'll be in and out in eleven minutes. Then Dale disappears and you resurface wherever you want, whenever you want."

He stared at the fake ID. Dale Schroeder looked back at him with his own terrified eyes.

Dylan, leaning against the wall with arms crossed, finally spoke. "And tonight?"

"Tonight," Roth said, "you stay dead. No social media, no old phones, no pity texts to ex-girlfriends. You're Schrödinger's millionaire until the money's in the trust. Alive and not alive at the same time."

Roth stood. Meeting over.

"One more thing." He handed over a plain black credit card with no name, no numbers on the front. "Unlimited until the wire hits. Use it like you're trying to get someone murdered. Hotels, jets, whatever keeps you moving. But every purchase has to look random and boring. No Lamborghinis. No strip clubs. Buy gas in small towns and groceries in big ones. Confusion is camouflage."

He took the card like it was radioactive.

Roth opened the steel door. Morning light sliced in, too bright.

"Flight leaves at nine. Someone will text you the gate from a burner. Don't miss it."

19

They stepped back into the alley. The door shut behind them with a finality that made his stomach drop.

Dylan exhaled. "Dale Schroeder. Has a ring to it."

He looked at the fake license again.

"Dale doesn't have cousins who text heart emojis," he said.

"Dale doesn't have friends who carry baseball bats either," Dylan replied, hefting the aluminum. "But here we are."

They walked toward the rental car parked two blocks away, hood already warming under the climbing sun.

Fourteen million dollars was twenty-four hours away.

So was the rest of his life.

Or whatever was left of it.

He slid the black card into the same pocket as the ticket, two pieces of plastic now deciding who he was allowed to be.

Dale Schroeder took his first breath.

And somewhere behind them, a white van turned the corner, slow and patient, waiting to see which way Dale decided to run.

Chapter 4
The Flight of Dale Schroeder

The jet was a six-seat Citation, paint chipped, tail number filed under some shell company in Delaware. The pilot never asked for names; he just nodded at the two men who climbed aboard looking like they'd slept in a dumpster.

Dylan took the rearmost seat, bat across his knees like carry-on luggage.

Our winner (now wearing a cheap flannel shirt stretched over a foam belly, spirit-gum sideburns, and a John Deere cap pulled low) sat sideways so the seatbelt didn't cut the prosthetic in half. Roth had done the makeup himself in a gas-station bathroom at dawn. The mirror had shown a stranger who looked forty-five going on sixty, the kind of guy who ate gas-station burritos and never won anything.

Perfect.

Takeoff was smooth, almost gentle. The plane climbed through a thin layer of morning clouds and leveled off above a carpet of cornfields that looked exactly like the life he was leaving behind.

Dylan leaned forward. "You okay under there, Dale?"

Dale's voice came out gravelly (Roth had made him practice a flat Iowa drawl for twenty minutes).

"Feels like I'm wearing someone else's skin."

"You are. That's the point."

The flight was only forty-three minutes gate-to-gate. Forty-three minutes to become someone else before the state of Iowa handed him the biggest novelty check in history.

He stared out the oval window. The ticket was in a new Ziplock, taped under the fake belly with medical tape. Every breath made the plastic crinkle against his real skin. A secret heartbeat.

His old phone (now wiped, battery out, wrapped in tinfoil like a burrito) sat in Dylan's backpack. The burner buzzed once. A single text from Roth:

Cameras are already at the claim center. Two local stations, one national. Stay in character. Do not smile. Dale doesn't know how.

He read it twice, then turned the burner off again.

Dylan watched him. "Remember: you're not claiming the money. Dale is. And Dale's having the worst day of his life."

"Copy that."

The plane banked, descending. The cornfields rushed up to meet them.

Touchdown was a small thump. A black Suburban idled on the tarmac (no plates, tinted windows). The co-pilot opened the door and warm Midwest air rolled in, smelling like fertilizer and second chances.

Roth was waiting beside the SUV, sunglasses reflecting the sky.

"Clock's ticking," he said. "Press conference is in ninety minutes whether you're there or not. We go in the back door, sign the forms, take the photo, leave. Eleven minutes total. You ready, Dale?"

Dale Schroeder adjusted his fake gut, felt the ticket shift against his skin, and nodded once.

"Let's get this over with."

They climbed into the Suburban. Doors shut like a bank vault.

As the car pulled away, Dale caught his reflection in the tinted window: puffy, tired, anonymous.

For the first time in thirty-six hours, he almost felt safe.

He didn't see the drone overhead, small and black against the sun, following them all the way to the claim center.

But someone else did.

Chapter 5
Eleven Minutes in Hell

The claim center was a low brick building behind a strip-mall that sold vaping supplies and tax-help. Nothing about it screamed "life-changing money," which was exactly why they used it.

Back door. Service corridor that smelled like bleach and old carpet. Roth led, Dale waddled two steps behind, Dylan brought up the rear carrying a cheap vinyl briefcase that held nothing but a legal pad and a lot of borrowed authority.

A lottery official in a navy suit met them with the exhausted smile of someone who'd already done this song-and-dance twice this year.

"Mr. Schroeder?" she asked, eyeing the prosthetic belly without blinking.

Dale grunted. Iowa drawl, flat and tired. "That's me."

"This way."

They walked past a janitor mopping the same spot over and over, past a fake potted plant that probably hid a camera. Into a conference room with no windows and one long table.

On the table: the oversized check made out to "Dale M. Schroeder" for $23,400,000.00. It looked like a prop from a bad game show.

A photographer stood ready. Two reporters hovered in the doorway until Roth stared them down and the door shut in their faces.

The official slid a stack of forms across.

"Sign wherever the yellow arrow is. Initial the tax pages. We already have the trust paperwork from counsel."

Dale's hand didn't shake. He'd practiced in the Suburban until the pen felt like an extension of the fake calluses Roth had glued to his fingers. Six signatures. Four initials. One thumbprint in blue ink.

Done.

The photographer raised the camera. "Mr. Schroeder, if you could hold the check—"

Dale gripped it with both meaty hands, stared straight into the lens with the dead eyes of a man who'd just buried his dog, and said nothing.

Flash. Flash. Done.

Roth was already moving. "Thank you, folks. Mr. Schroeder has a prior engagement."

Out the same corridor, past the janitor who was now mopping a different spot, back door, into the waiting Suburban.

Eleven minutes exactly.

The second the door slammed, Dale ripped off the fake sideburns and let out a sound halfway between laugh and sob.

Dylan slapped the seat in front of him. "We fucking did it!"

Roth didn't smile. He was looking at his phone.

"We've got a problem."

Dale's blood turned to slush. "What kind of problem?"

Roth turned the screen.

A photo, taken from directly above the claim center roof less than five minutes ago: Dale holding the giant check, face perfectly clear despite the hat and prosthetics.

Underneath, already posted to a local Facebook group with 47k members:

EASTSIDE WINNER IS THIS GUY. I KNOW HIM. NAME IS NOT DALE.

Comments exploding:

That's definitely [redacted] from the Eastside apartments

He used to date my sister

Someone tag his mom lol

DM for his new number $$$

The post had 2,100 shares in four minutes.

Roth met his eyes in the rear-view.

"Change of plans. Airport's burned. We drive."

Dale stared at the screen until the letters blurred.

Eleven minutes to become the richest man in the state.

Less than five to become the most hunted.

He looked out the window as the Suburban merged onto the highway doing ninety.

Somewhere behind them, half the internet was already turning into bloodhounds.

Dale Schroeder was dead.

And the real him had exactly zero places left to hide.

Chapter 6
The Highway
Becomes a Runway

Roth drove. No GPS, no phone maps, just muscle memory and a paper atlas spread across the passenger seat like a war plan.

Dylan rode shotgun, bat across his lap again, eyes on the mirrors.

Our winner (no longer Dale, not yet anyone else) sat in the back with the seatbelt cutting into the foam gut he hadn't dared peel off yet.

The first hour was pure silence except for the engine and the occasional crackle of Roth's police scanner app running through a hidden tablet.

"...possible sighting of the Eastside winner heading west on I-80, white Suburban, unknown plates..."

Roth killed the feed.

"They're guessing," he said. "For now."

The second hour the sky turned the color of a healing bruise. Corn gave way to more corn. Every overpass felt like a sniper's nest.

Dylan finally spoke. "Where the hell are we actually going?"

"Place I keep for clients who need to disappear before they disappear," Roth answered. "Old grain elevator outside Kearney, Nebraska. Converted the top two floors. No address, no utilities in my name, Starlink dish hidden in a fake silo. You can see twenty miles in every direction. Nothing gets within a mile without us knowing."

Our winner found his voice. "And then?"

"Then we wait for the wire to clear, which takes three to five business days. After that you pick a continent and I make the rest of the world forget you were ever born."

He stared at the back of Roth's head. "You've done this before."

"More than you want to know about."

The third hour the burner phone Roth kept in the console buzzed once. A text from a number that showed only as a single period.

Roth read it and his jaw flexed.

"Change of plans again."

Dylan turned. "Define change."

"Someone just offered fifty thousand dollars on the dark web for a clean photo of the winner's real face. Bounty goes up every hour it isn't filled."

He felt the foam belly suddenly weigh a thousand pounds.

Dylan whistled low. "That's marketing."

Roth took an exit with no sign, just a gravel road that disappeared between two walls of corn.

"From here we go dark. Phones in the Faraday bag. We're ghosts until further notice."

The Suburban bounced down the gravel, dust pluming behind like a smoke signal no one was supposed to see.

He leaned his forehead against the cool window and watched the last sliver of daylight bleed out.

Fourteen million dollars was already his.

Freedom was apparently extra.

The corn closed in behind them, swallowing the road whole.

Somewhere out there, half the country was refreshing the same Facebook post, zooming in on the blurry photo of a man who no longer existed, trying to recognize the eyes they used to know.

He closed them.

The madness wasn't winning anymore.

It had already won.

Chapter 7
The Silo

The grain elevator rose out of the dark like a concrete cathedral abandoned by God and agriculture. Six stories of brutalist cylinder, graffiti long faded, windows shot out years ago. Roth killed the headlights a quarter mile out and coasted the rest of the way on momentum and memory.

They parked inside the ground-level loading bay. A steel door the size of a house rolled shut behind them with a clang that echoed up the hollow spine of the building.

Roth hit a breaker. One string of LED shop lights flickered on, revealing a freight elevator that looked like it had survived the Cold War.

"Top floor," he said.

The ride up was slow and loud enough to wake the dead. When the gate rattled open, the space was nothing like he expected.

Polished concrete floors. A wall of blacked-out monitors. A kitchen ripped from a luxury tiny-home catalog. One corner gym, another corner bed the size of his old apartment. In the center: a single leather chair facing a sixty-inch screen showing sixteen live drone feeds of the surrounding prairie.

Dylan let out a low whistle. "You've been holding out on us, Roth."

"Clients pay for peace of mind," Roth answered, already shrugging off his jacket. "This is where I deliver it."

Our winner peeled off the foam belly at last, wincing as the tape took skin with it. The empty Ziplock that had once held the ticket dropped to the counter with a soft, meaningless slap. He stared at the rectangle of nothing inside it. The real ticket was gone: surrendered hours ago in that windowless room in Des Moines, scanned, stamped, locked away forever in whatever vault the state keeps for proof that miracles actually happen. All that remained was plastic shaped like the thing that had detonated his life.

He let the empty bag fall into the trash. No ceremony. Just the quiet sound of letting go of the last physical piece of who he used to be.

Roth poured three fingers of something brown into heavy glasses and handed one over without asking.

"Drink. Then shower. Then we talk endgame."

The shower was glass and rain-head and hotter than hell. He stood under it until the water ran cold, watching fake tan and spirit gum circle the drain like the last of his old face.

When he came out in borrowed sweatpants, Dylan was at the monitor wall, bat finally set aside, eating cereal straight from the box.

Roth sat at a desk that looked like mission control, fingers flying.

"Good news and bad news," he said without looking up.

"Bad first."

"Someone doxxed your full name, address, mother's maiden name, and the high-school mascot to a site with two million daily users. It's the top trending topic in the Midwest. Congratulations, you're Patient Zero of a viral manhunt."

He felt the floor tilt.

"Good news?"

"The money wired an hour ago. Fourteen point two cleared the Caymans, bounced through three more trusts, and is currently sleeping in a numbered account in Liechtenstein. It's untouchable. Even I can't find it anymore, and I built the maze."

Dylan raised his cereal box in salute. "So we're rich and radioactive."

"Exactly," Roth said. "Which is why we leave the country tonight."

"Tonight?"

Roth spun the chair to face him.

"Private Gulfstream, small strip thirty miles west. Flight plan filed to Reykjavik under a medical emergency for a burn victim who needs specialized care. That's you. Facial bandages, wheelchair, the works. From Iceland we hop to wherever you want. New passports waiting in a locker at Keflavik. After that you live quiet for a year, maybe two, then resurface as whoever you decide to become."

He stared at the monitors. One feed showed a convoy of pickup trucks on a distant county road, headlights cutting through the dark like wolves.

"How many people are out there right now?"

"Hard to say. Hundreds. Maybe thousands by morning. Some want selfies. Some want GoFundMe. A few want kidneys. One posted a photo of a rifle scope and your old apartment door."

Dylan crunched cereal louder. "So we're doing the burn-victim thing?"

"We're doing the burn-victim thing."

Roth stood.

"Chopper picks us up on the roof in forty-one minutes. Pack light. One bag. No souvenirs."

He looked around the sterile fortress that had kept him safe for exactly two hours and felt nothing.

Dylan clapped him on the shoulder. "Come on, millionaire. Time to go die so you can start living."

Roth killed the lights.

"Clock just moved up. Roof. Now."

They ran.

Unfindable

The madness wasn't chasing him anymore.

He was finally outrunning it.

Or so he thought.

Chapter 8
Rooftop, 2:47 a.m

The night was so clear the Milky Way looked like spilled sugar. Wind whipped across the silo roof, cold enough to bite through the sweatpants. A single red chem-light glowed in Roth's hand; the only thing the incoming pilot would see.

The helicopter came in low and fast, no navigation lights, just the black silhouette of a Bell 407 slicing the stars. It hovered ten feet above the gravel roof, rotor-wash blasting them with dust and the smell of jet fuel.

A side door slid open. A figure in a flight suit and night-vision goggles waved them in.

Roth went first, then Dylan, then our winner, handed up like luggage. The moment his feet left the roof the chopper banked hard and climbed, Nebraska shrinking beneath them in seconds.

Inside, the cabin lights were blood-red. Someone shoved a bundle of white gauze and medical tape into his lap.

"Start wrapping," the co-pilot shouted over the engine. "Face, neck, hands. Leave a slit for eyes and mouth. You're the burn patient now."

He tore open the packages with shaking fingers. Dylan helped, winding the gauze tight, turning him into a faceless mummy. The fake pain was perfect cover; he actually winced when the tape pulled skin.

Roth was already on a satellite phone, voice calm. "Package airborne. ETA Keflavik zero-six-thirty Zulu. Have the medevac team standing by with the chair and the paperwork."

He caught Roth's eye through the slit in the bandages.

Roth gave one short nod. So far, so good.

The chopper flew nap-of-the-earth, skimming treetops and power lines, staying off radar. Forty minutes of stomach-lurching turns and sudden climbs. Nobody spoke. The only sound was rotor blades and the occasional crackle of encrypted radio traffic.

Then the pilot's voice, flat and urgent: "Traffic, eleven o'clock low. Two heat signatures climbing fast. Drones."

Roth leaned forward. "Ours?"

"Negative. Commercial quadcopters, weaponized. Someone's paying top dollar for night footage."

Dylan swore. "Can we outrun them?"

"Not the point," the pilot said. "They just want one clear shot of the passenger. After that they cash out and go home."

Our winner felt the bandages go damp under his eyes; sweat or tears, impossible to tell.

Roth pulled a flare gun from a seat pocket, loaded a red cartridge.

"Open the door."

The co-pilot slid it. Wind screamed in.

Roth leaned out, aimed straight up, and fired. The flare burst high and bright, a second sun. The pursuing drones veered, blinded by the magnesium bloom, rotors stuttering as their cameras white-balanced to death.

The chopper dove hard left, dropped into a ravine, and flew fifty feet above a river that reflected nothing but darkness.

Thirty seconds later the pilot's voice again, almost amused.

"Lost them. Kids with toys versus military countermeasures. No contest."

The door slid shut. The cabin fell quiet again.

He sat back, heart hammering against the gauze, tasting copper through the slit in the bandages.

Dylan's voice, low beside him: "We're not even out of the country yet and people are already trying to kill us with camera drones."

He laughed. One short, muffled bark that hurt his taped face.

"Fourteen million dollars," he said, voice distorted and strange. "Cheaper than I thought."

Roth didn't laugh. He was watching the satellite phone like it might bite.

A new message blinked.

Single line.

Nice try with the bandages.

See you in Iceland.

No sender. Just a photo attached: the helicopter's tail number, crystal clear, taken from above the flare burst.

Roth looked at it for a long second, then powered the phone all the way off and pulled the battery.

He met our winner's eyes through the gauze slit.

"Change of destination," he said. "We're not going to Iceland anymore."

The helicopter banked north, chasing the last edge of night.

Somewhere beneath the bandages, the millionaire-in-hiding closed his eyes and waited for the next lie that might keep him breathing.

Chapter 9
Somewhere Over Canada, 4:12 a.m.

The pilot killed the transponder, dropped to two hundred feet above endless black pine, and flew by GPS and moonlight alone.

Roth finally spoke the new plan in a voice so low the rotor noise almost swallowed it.

"We're going to a strip outside Thunder Bay. Dirt, unlit, no tower. Belongs to a bush pilot who owes me his life twice. From there we switch to a floatplane registered to a dead man. After that, we cross Hudson Bay under visual flight rules, no flight plan filed. Final destination: a fishing lodge on the east coast of James Bay. No roads in or out for a hundred and fifty miles. Population: eight Inuit elders and one sat phone that only works when the tide's right."

Dylan exhaled through his teeth. "So basically the Arctic witness-protection program."

"Exactly."

Unfindable

Our winner (now just a gauze-wrapped shape with a heartbeat) tried to process it.

From a convenience-store ticket to a Cree fishing camp in less than seventy-two hours.

It felt less like escape and more like being erased.

Roth handed him a pill and a bottle of water.

"Sleep. Next four hours are going to hurt."

He swallowed without asking what it was. The cabin lights dimmed to red. The engines became a lullaby.

He dreamed of white vans and camera flashes and a giant novelty check with his real face on it.

He woke to the floatplane's props winding down on black water.

Dawn was a thin bruise on the horizon. Ice fog drifted off the bay like cigarette smoke. The air that rushed in when the door opened was sharp enough to cut lungs.

A woman in a caribou parka and a rifle slung easy stood on the dock. Mid-fifties, braid streaked with grey, eyes that had seen everything and forgiven almost none of it.

Roth greeted her in Cree. She answered in English.

"You brought trouble," she said, nodding at the bandaged figure.

"The kind that pays triple," Roth replied.

She considered, then shrugged. "Money keeps the generator running."

She helped him out of the plane. His legs had forgotten how to work. The dock creaked under new weight.

Inside the lodge: Woodstove already roaring, coffee thick as tar, a table made from an old dogsled.

Eight elders glanced up from their card game, nodded once, went back to their hands.

He was clearly not the first ghost they'd hosted.

The woman (her name was Maggie) peeled the bandages off his face like removing a death mask. The cold air on raw skin felt like salvation.

She studied him for a long second.

"You look like someone who died and forgot to lie down," she said.

He laughed. Couldn't help it. The sound scared a raven off the windowsill.

Roth spread a paper map on the table, the first paper map he'd seen in days.

"Welcome to the edge of the world," he said. "No cell towers, no Starlink, no drones. Sat phone only works two hours a day when the satellite feels generous. Closest road is two hundred kilometers south and closed six months of the year. You stay here until the heat dies or the money runs out; whichever comes second."

Dylan dropped into a chair, finally set the baseball bat down for good, and accepted a mug of coffee the size of a soup bowl.

"How long are we talking?"

Roth didn't answer right away. He was looking out the window at the endless white and black of James Bay.

"Could be a month. Could be never," he said finally. "Internet forgets fast, but it never deletes. Your face is already in too many training datasets. One clear photo at an airport in five years and the wrong AI flags you. Some people live with that. Some don't."

Silence settled, thick as the woodsmoke.

Maggie broke it. "There's a spare cabin. Heat, propane, books, rifle, snowshoes. You'll earn your keep chopping wood and checking the nets. No internet, no news, no mirrors for the first week. After that, we see what kind of man walks out of the quiet."

He looked around the room: eight elders who already knew his real name and didn't care, Dylan half-asleep with his head on the table, Roth cleaning a satellite phone with a toothbrush like it was a firearm, and Maggie watching him with the calm of someone who'd buried husbands and still got up to fish.

He felt something loosen in his chest for the first time since the numbers had matched.

Outside, the northern lights flickered on like God switching the stage lights to low.

He was fourteen million dollars rich, legally dead, and as far off the grid as a human being could get without actually leaving the planet.

The madness wasn't gone.

It just finally had nowhere left to run.

He picked up the axe by the door.

Time to start chopping.

Chapter 10
Thirty-Seven
Days of Silence

The first week he forgot his own name.

He woke before light, chopped wood until his palms blistered, set nets through ice thick as guilt, ate caribou stew and bannock and whatever the elders won at cards.

No one used his old name. Maggie called him "Napa" (boy) even though he was twenty-seven. The elders called him nothing at all; they just pointed at the woodpile when it was low.

He slept ten hours a night and still felt tired.

The quiet was so complete he could hear his own pulse in his ears.

Day eight he tried to remember what his apartment smelled like. Couldn't.

Day twelve he caught himself smiling at a raven that stole his mittens and didn't know why.

Day twenty-one he realized he hadn't checked for white vans in three weeks.

On day thirty-seven the sat phone caught a signal for exactly nine minutes.

Roth's voice came through like gravel dragged over ice.

"You still breathing?"

"Yeah."

"Good. World moved on. Your face is off the front page. Replaced by a senator and his mistress and a missing submarine. You're officially yesterday's meme."

He pressed the phone harder to his ear, suddenly starving for any voice that wasn't wind or woodstove.

"And the money?"

"Still growing. Quietly. You're up another six figures in index funds. You could buy this entire bay if you wanted."

He looked out the window at the endless white. "I don't."

Silence for a beat.

"You ready to come back?" Roth asked.

He thought about the axe calluses, the way Maggie now called him "Napa" with affection instead of correction, the way the northern lights felt like they were dancing just for him.

"No," he said.

Another beat.

"Didn't think so," Roth said, almost gentle. "Call when you are. Or don't. Your call, millionaire."

The signal died.

He set the phone down and walked outside without a jacket. The cold slapped him awake the way it had every morning for five weeks.

Dylan was on the ice, helping one of the elders fix a snow machine. He looked up, grinned, and flipped him the bird; their new hello.

He waved back.

Later, when the sun finally crawled above the trees for its brief winter appearance, he stood on the frozen bay and looked south.

Somewhere down there were fourteen million dollars, a thousand new followers, cousins with heart emojis, drones with cameras, and a version of himself screaming in an apartment that no longer existed.

Up here there was just wind, ice, and eight old men who'd decided he was worth teaching how to read the weather in the snow.

He took one breath that tasted like pine and minus thirty and felt something settle into place.

The madness hadn't lost.

It had simply run out of room.

He turned back toward the lodge, boots crunching a path that would be gone by morning.

Behind him, the northern lights flared green and purple, bright enough to cast shadows.

He didn't look back.

He didn't need to.

The ticket was gone, the money was invisible, and the man who'd won it all was finally, perfectly, unfindable.

Even to himself.

End.

About the Author

George Hatcher's life is a testament to second chances. With a formal education that ended in the ninth grade, he has navigated a life of extreme highs and devastating lows, learning his most profound lessons not in a classroom, but through trial and error.

The first half of his life was a whirlwind of entrepreneurial ventures—some successful, others leading to catastrophic failures and, ultimately, prison. Through it all, the one constant, the anchor in every storm, has been his wife, Molly. Their 60-year marriage is the bedrock upon which the second half of his life—one of stability, peace, and prolific writing—was built.

As a passionate storyteller with over two dozen books to his name, George writes from a place of hard-won experience. He explores themes of love, loss, failure, and forgiveness, not as a theorist, but as a man who has lived them. He believes his greatest mistakes have been his most profound teachers and shares his story with unflinching honesty.

He currently resides in Rancho Mirage, California, with Molly, their three cats, and a macaw named Peaches. Now devoted entirely to his craft, George invites readers to join him on a remarkable journey that proves beauty isn't found in perfection, but in the strength it takes to repair what is broken.

A longer bio is available on his website: http://georgehatcher.com/bio/bio.html